1/05

**THREE RIVERS
PUBLIC LIBRARY**
www.three-rivers-library.org
MINOOKA BRANCH LIBRARY
MINOOKA, IL 60447
815-467-1600

DEMCO

Mortimer's ABCs

Karen Bryant-Mole

Gareth Stevens Publishing
A WORLD ALMANAC EDUCATION GROUP COMPANY

Mortimer's Fun with Words

For a free color catalog describing Gareth Stevens' list of high-quality books and multimedia programs, call 1-800-542-2595 (USA) or 1-800-461-9120 (Canada). Gareth Stevens Publishing's Fax: (414) 332-3567.

Library of Congress Cataloging-in-Publication Data available upon request from publisher. Fax: (414) 332-3567 for the attention of the Publishing Records Department.

ISBN 0-8368-2750-3

This North American edition first published in 2000 by
Gareth Stevens Publishing
A World Almanac Education Group Company
330 West Olive Street, Suite 100
Milwaukee, WI 53212 USA

This edition © 2000 by Gareth Stevens, Inc. Original © BryantMole Books, 1999. First published in 1999 by Evans Brothers Limited, 2A Portman Mansions, Chiltern Street, London W1M 1LE, United Kingdom. Additional end matter © 2000 by Gareth Stevens, Inc.

Created by Karen Bryant-Mole
Photographs by Zul Mukhida
Designed by Jean Wheeler
Teddy bear by Merrythought Ltd.

Printed in the United States of America

1 2 3 4 5 6 7 8 9 04 03 02 01 00

contents

a is for **alligator**

Mortimer's alligator is his favorite toy animal.

b

b is for **butterfly**, and **c** is for **camera**

c

What a beautiful butterfly!
Mortimer can take a picture of it with his camera.

d e

d is for
dinosaur, and
e is for **egg**

Mortimer thinks dinosaurs are delightful.
Be extra careful with that egg, Mortimer!

f is for **fish**

Mortimer wants to make friends with this fish.

g h

g is for **guitar**, and **h** is for **horse**

g

h

Mortimer is good at playing the guitar. He is playing a happy tune for his horse.

Mortimer thinks insects are interesting.

j k

j is for **jam**, and **k** is for **kangaroo**

Mortimer's jam is in a jar.

A kangaroo keeps its baby in a pouch.

l is for **lollipop**

Mortimer likes to lick a lollipop.

m is for **mirror**, and **n** is for **necklace**

Can you see Mortimer in the mirror?
He is wearing a colorful new necklace.

o is for **octopus**

This octopus often visits Mortimer.

Mortimer is wearing a pair of pajamas.
He will sleep quietly under the quilt.

r is for **rocket**

Mortimer has a red rocket.

s is for **sand**, and
t is for **turtle**

Mortimer is sitting in a sandbox.
The turtle is taking a long time to get there.

u

u is for
umbrella

Mortimer is sitting under an umbrella.

V W

v is for **vegetables**, and w is for **watch**

Mortimer has a variety of vegetables.
His watch tells him when it is time to eat!

box ends in x

Can you find a number six
on Mortimer's toy box?

y

y is for **yo-yo**

Mortimer's yellow yo-yo goes up and down.

Mortimer likes the zebra at the zoo.

All the ABCs

Mortimer wants to review all the letters of the alphabet.

a b c d e f
g h i j k
l m n o p
q r s t u
v w x y z

Can you name each letter?

glossary/index

alligator — an animal that lives in the water and has big, sharp teeth and scaly skin 4

delightful — very nice 6

insect — an animal, such as a butterfly or grasshopper, that has six legs and three main body parts 9

jam — a thick, sweet spread made from fruit and sugar 10

kangaroo — an animal from Australia that hops with its strong back legs 10

octopus — an animal with eight legs and a soft, rounded body that lives in the ocean 13

quilt — a thick blanket filled with padding 14

turtle — a slow-moving animal that likes land and water and has a hard shell that covers its body 16

yo-yo — a toy with string wrapped around the center that moves up and down as you play with it 20

videos

Dr. Seuss ABCs. (Sony Music Distribution)

Miracle of Mozart – ABCs. (Tapeworm)

Sesame Street – The Alphabet Jungle Game. (Sony Wonder)